Once Upon A Time there was a woman named Teresa. She was kind and friendly, and helped everyone in her community. She used to sing and say, 'How good and pleasant it is, when brothers and sisters live in unity!'

Teresa used to read newspapers, daily. Every day, Teresa would read articles with headings like 'Overworked staff fall sick', 'Children are victims of evil parents' and 'Beggar set on fire'.

The articles informed how employers were overworking their staff, parents were rude and unkind to their children, and citizens were selfish and mean to people in need.

Reading these articles made Teresa feel sad and angry. Still, she continued singing and saying to her neighbours, 'How good and pleasant it is, when brothers and sisters live in unity!'

But one day as Teresa read another article headed 'Beggar set on fire' she began crying and her chest started hurting. She was overwhelmed with sadness and anger.

She tried to sing and say, 'How good and pleasant it is, when brothers and sisters live in unity!', but she couldn't, she was consumed with sadness and anger.

Teresa didn't talk about her feelings, because she didn't like feeling sad or angry. So, she hid her emotions and kept her thoughts to herself.

'Why, Why!' 'I wish - I wish!' 'I don't like - I don't like!' 'If only they would!' Her emotions and thoughts became a problem. Teresa began to experience depression, intense anger, and worry.

Teresa wanted a break from her emotions and thoughts, and needed to relax. She remembered that alcohol could alter one's thoughts and emotions, and encourage relaxation. So, she drank some wine.

The wine made her feel merry, and her thoughts were no longer a problem - she didn't feel depressed, angry or worried!

Teresa began to drink wine daily, because she felt sad and angry, every day.

Teresa's neighbours noticed lots of empty wine bottles in Teresa's recycling bin. Seven bottles of wine filled her bin at the end of each week! They realised Teresa was drinking a bottle of wine every day, and they began to worry about her.

One day a neighbour asked, 'Why do you drink wine every day?'

'I've got a "Fish in my Head!", Teresa snapped.

'What do you mean 'You've got a "Fish in your Head'?', the neighbour quizzed.

'I've got a 'Fish in my Head' that is sad and angry, and worries. So, it needs to drink wine to feel happy and relax', Teresa explained.

When Teresa drank wine she became fearless and courageous. She spoke angrily about the things the 'Fish in her Head' didn't like.

'You overwork your staff! You're rude and unkind to your children! You're selfish and mean to people in need!', she would shout, and blamed them for the wickedness in the world.

'You're evil! You should love your brothers, your neighbours, and your children, as yourself. There is no other importance greater than these', she would bellow.

'You're a drunkard! A waste of space! An alcoholic!', people jeered.

Teresa began having accidents whilst she was drunk. Sometimes she would trip and fall over, other times she would walk into doors.

Teresa's neighbours began to worry even more about her.

'Teresa! Don't you know your body is a temple for your precious life? You're destroying your temple, and so you are destroying your life', a kind neighbour advised.

'You're acting unwisely, Teresa! Stop getting drunk with wine. That is dissipation. You need to start singing again, and making melody in your heart and with life', another caring neighbour advised.

'It's not me who's destroying my temple! And, I'm not acting unwisely! I've got a "Fish in my Head" that is sad and angry, and needs to drink wine to feel happy and relax', Teresa moaned.

Teresa didn't like having accidents. She began to worry about her excessive drinking of wine, and got angry with the 'Fish in her Head'.

'Go away! Take your sadness, anger and worry to someone else!', she bellowed at the 'Fish in her Head'.

'No! I won't go away! Employers are overworking their staff, parents are rude and unkind to their children, and citizens are selfish and mean to people in need!', the 'Fish in her Head' snapped back.

She agreed with the 'Fish in her Head', but she didn't like having accidents, because of her excessive drinking of wine.

'Oh, I do what I don't want to do! But, it's not me that's doing it. It's the badness that lives inside me,' Teresa affirmed.

One day the Fish was feeling very sad and angry.

It kept thinking 'Employers overwork their staff, parents are rude and unkind to their children, and citizens are selfish and mean to people in need. 'Why, Why!' 'I wish - I wish!' 'I don't like - I don't like!' 'If only they would.'

Teresa desperately wanted to help the 'Fish in her Head' to feel happy and relaxed. She needed to go shopping to get wine for the Fish.

Teresa's thoughts were so focused on getting the wine, that she wasn't paying attention as she crossed the road. She stepped out onto the road, and a car knocked her over!

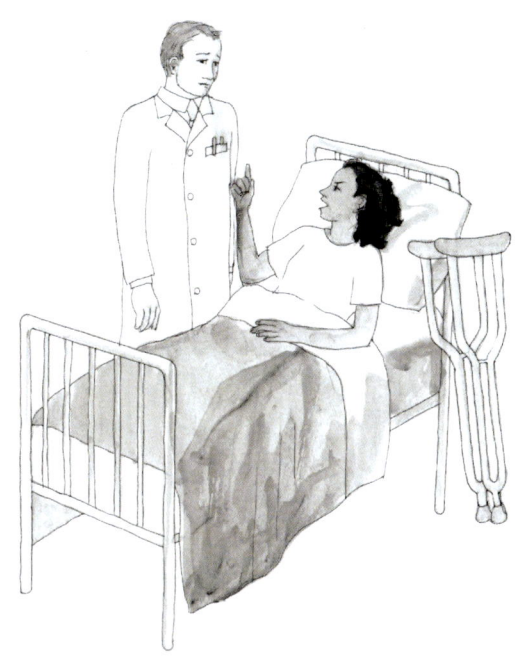

Teresa was rushed to hospital!

She had a broken leg and two broken ribs.

'There's a risk of your ribs piercing your lungs, and that could be fatal. So you need to stay in hospital. You also need to learn how to use crutches and manage your alcohol problem', the emergency doctor said.

'I haven't got an alcohol problem! I've got a 'Fish in my Head' that needs alcohol to feel happy and relaxed', Teresa tried to explain, but he didn't understand.

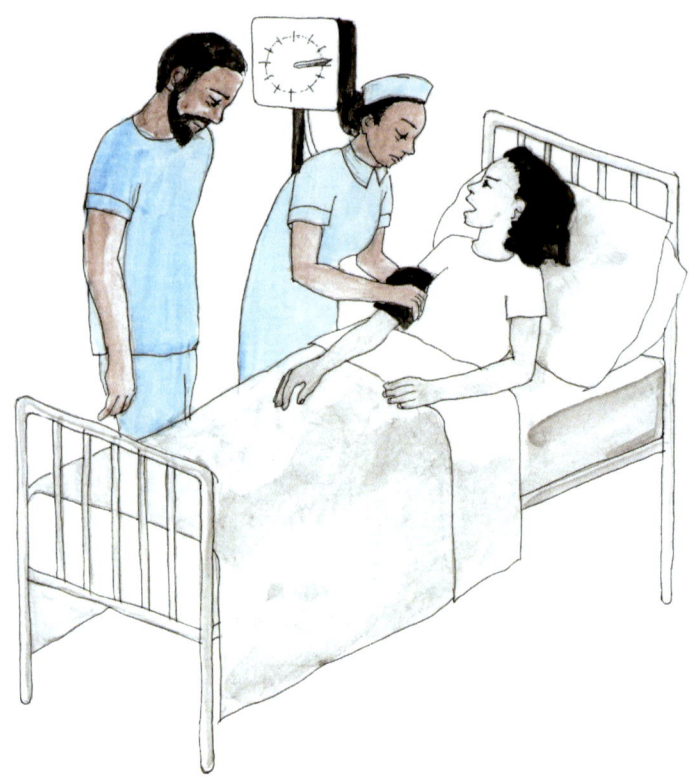

The Fish in Teresa's head was angry and scared of being in hospital. It could see that the nurses and doctors were overworked and not alert.

'You should work for no more than six days, and on the seventh day rest, to be refreshed. Leave me alone! You're half asleep and don't know what you're doing!', Teresa shouted at the overworked staff.

One night as Teresa lay in the hospital bed she heard a voice say, 'Teresa, let peace be with you. Let your heart not be troubled, or afraid'.

She felt at peace and comforted, but was unsure if she could trust what she heard was real.

But the words were 'powerful and sharper than a sword', and they 'pierced her soul, spirit, and joints, separating her from her own thoughts and fear'.

The following morning a friendly doctor visited Teresa. 'Teresa, let peace be with you. Let your heart not be troubled, or afraid', he said.

These were the same words Teresa had heard the night before!

'There is no 'Fish in your Head'. You drink alcohol because of your sadness and anger. You were knocked over by a car because you were drunk, and full of worry. You're fortunate to be alive - you were saved! I'm going to refer you for counselling', he said.

Teresa wanted to be angry with the doctor and say, 'How dare you! My sadness, anger and life are none of your business!'

But she heard the same voice, she heard the night before say, 'Listen to his advice, and accept his instruction, so that you may gain wisdom in the future'.

Teresa attended counselling. She spoke about the 'Fish in her Head's' sadness, anger and worries.

'The Fish doesn't like the way people treat each other. Employers overworking their staff... Parents are rude and unkind to their children... And citizens are selfish and mean to people in need. 'I love you!', they proclaim, but they don't know love. If they did, they would love their brothers and sisters affectionately, with respect and give preference to each other', she ranted.

'What do you think you can do about the "Fish in your Head"'s', sadness, anger and worries about the way people treat each other?' The counsellor asked.

The "Fish in my Head" needs to forgive them, because they don't know what they're doing', Teresa replied.

The Fish started forgiving people for their unloving behaviour, and stopped allowing feelings of sadness, anger and worry, be problems.

It no longer needed wine to feel happy and relaxed, and began singing 'Be kind to one another, tender-heartedly, forgiving one another, as the Spirit's forgiven me!'

Teresa stopped shouting at people and blaming them for the wickedness in the world, because the 'Fish in her Head' realised that sometimes it behaved unlovingly, and would like to be forgiven.

Teresa returned to being kind and friendly, helping everyone in her community.

'How good and pleasant it is, when brothers and sisters live in unity!', she began singing and saying again.

'Our kind, friendly Teresa is back! She's singing again!', her neighbours rejoiced.

At the next counselling session the counsellor asked, 'What worries does the "Fish in your Head" need to talk about today?'

'The "Fish in my Head" doesn't have any worries to talk about, and I haven't needed to drink wine to help it to feel happy and relaxed. The Fish is like a new creation. The old one has passed away, and become new!', Teresa replied with happiness.

'That's Good News! You trusted the Spirit with all your heart, and not your own. Well done!', the counsellor praised.

Teresa trained to be a Alcoholic Support Worker and began serving people. She listened to their stories, comforted them, and helped people to help themselves.

She realised from her experience that people didn't drink, because they were 'drunkards', 'a waste of space', or 'alcoholics'. She recognised that people drank excessively because their lives seemed unbearable to them, and they were unable to deal with their emotions.

'You're amazing! You're a brilliant teacher! You've change our lives!,' the people she served carolled.

'It is not me that's amazing, or who has changed your life! It's the Spirit within me that reminds me to do good and to share. It's pleased with such actions', Teresa rejoiced.

Teresa served for many years, always singing and saying, 'How good and pleasant it is, when brothers and sisters live in unity!'

And she lived Happily Ever After.

THE END

Acknowledgements

God - The Almighty Father:

You are the reason why I am here. You are the reason for this contribution, and I live with constant thanks for the richness of my Life.

Scriptures that informed the wisdom of the characters in this fairy tale (New King James Version).

Psalm 133:1
Behold, how good and how pleasant *it is,* For brethren to dwell together in unity!

Mark 12:31
And the second, like *it, is* this: 'You shall love your neighbour as yourself.' There is no other commandment greater than these.'

1 Corinthians 3: 16-17
Do you not know that you are the temple of God and *that* the Spirit of God dwells in you? If anyone defiles the temple of God, God will destroy him. For the temple of God is holy, which *temple* you are.

Ephesians 5: 17-19
Therefore do not be unwise, but understand what the will of the Lord *is.* And do not be drunk with wine, in which is dissipation; but be filled with the Spirit, speaking to one another in psalms and hymns and spiritual songs, singing and making melody in your heart to the Lord,

Romans 7:2
Now if I do what I will not *to do,* it is no longer I who do it, but sin that dwells in me.

John 14:27
Peace I leave with you, my peace I give unto you: not as the world giveth, give I unto you. Let not your heart be troubled, neither let it be afraid.

Hebrews 4:12
For the word of God *is* living and powerful, and sharper than any two-edged sword, piercing even to the division of soul and spirit, and of joints and marrow, and is a discerner of the thoughts and intents of the heart.

Proverbs 19:20
Listen to counsel and receive instruction, That you may be wise in your latter days.

Romans 12:10
Be kindly affectionate to one another with brotherly love, in honour giving preference to one another.

Ephesians 4:32
And be kind to one another, tenderhearted, forgiving one another, even as God in Christ forgave you.

Proverbs 3:5
Trust in the LORD with all your heart, And lean not on your own understanding.

2 Corinthians 5:17
Therefore, if anyone is in Christ, he is a new creation. The old has passed away; behold, the new has come.